TEACH ME HOW TO PRAY

PRAYING USING THE SCRIPTURES

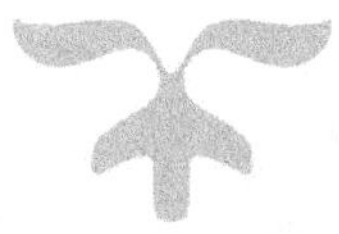

ROSE SHIKU

www.effectiveglobaltraining.com

All rights reserved. No part of this publication may be reproduced, transmitted, or distributed or transmitted in any form or by any means including photocopying, recording or other electronic or mechanical methods without the prior written permission of Effective Global Training, except in the case of brief quotations embodied in critical reviews and certain other noncommercial uses permitted by copyright law.

ISBN: 9798573502250
© 2020 Effective Global Training

Dedicated to

Benson and Rahab Mwangi

You taught me my first prayer.

PREFACE

Luke 11:1 says, now it came to pass, as He was praying in a certain place, when He ceased, that one of his disciples said to Him, "Lord teach us to pray." The disciples desired to learn the art of prayer just as Jesus prayed.

Jesus answered them and said when you pray, say.

Our Father in heaven (approaching the throne of God as a son and daughter)

Hallowed be Your name (Holy is your name depicting honor and reverence to God)

Your kingdom come; your will be done on earth as *it is* in heaven (your desires over our life be fulfilled)

Give us day by day our daily bread (daily provision)

And forgive us our sins (forgive us for our wrongdoing and where we have not walked in your ways)

For we also forgive everyone who is indebted to us (we in turn need to forgive as we have been forgiven)

And do not lead us into temptation, But deliver us from the evil one (wisdom to know and choose what is right vs what is wrong and protect us from the evil one)

Prayer is communication with God, and just as the disciples desired to learn, prayer can be taught. In this book, you will not only learn to pray but to pray strategically using scriptures. This book is for the new believer, leader, mother, father, child, and student, that desires to commune with God every day and through every season.

Prayer is a relationship with God. It builds, shapes, molds, and guides us. This book is designed to help you.

-Pray using the scriptures
-Transform your prayer life.
-Develop a more vital and consistent prayer life.
-Develop a deeper relationship with God as you apply scriptures to your prayers.

Praying the scriptures is essential and vital because God's word is steadfast and endures forever (Isaiah 40:8). His word will never fade away (Mathew 24:35). When you pray the scriptures, you create a case with evidence and proof that what you are praying for is possible. His word does not return unto Him void, but it accomplishes that which it was sent (Isaiah 55:10-11). God watches over his word to perform it (Jeremiah 1:12), so when you pray, he watches over your prayer to perform it. The word of God is alive (Hebrews 4:12), and so will your prayers be brought to life.

If we are required to live according to the word of God as it is written in Psalms 119:9, then we should pray according to this word. When we pray Gods word, we pray what is right, accurate, dependable, and trustworthy (Psalms 33:4)

Prayer is communication with God, and just as the disciples desired to learn, prayer can be taught.

<u>WHY PRAY</u>

The Bible tells us in Luke 18:1 that we ought to pray and not faint meaning prayer is an all-time thing, and we should not get weary of prayer.

Prayer is communion with God; it is where we make our requests known to God (Philippians 4:6). Communion means to have a relationship and intimacy. To achieve intimacy and relationship one must be intentional and consistent.

Prayer is a lifestyle. Jesus prayed regularly (Luke 5:16), and there are times he prayed all night (Luke 6:12).

Prayer is essential in our lives. When we look at the life of Jesus, he often retreated to a private place to pray (Mark 1:35). He prayed at pivotal moments of his life. Before his ministry began, he went for 40 days of prayer and fasting (Luke 4:1-13). He prayed the night before he died (Luke 22:41-46)

Make prayer an integral part of your life. Jesus ministry depended on prayer. His disciples may have desired to be taught to perform the miracles they saw Jesus perform, but they desired to learn how to pray.

CONTENTS

<u>THANKSGIVING</u>

The Bible tells us in Psalms 100 to enter his gates with thanksgiving and his courts with praise. We approach the throne of God, and enter the presence of the Almighty God, with praises and thanksgiving. In our human nature, we value appreciation, so it is likewise with our Heavenly Father. Giving thanks is an expression of gratitude, it is acknowledging Gods work in you and in your life. Giving thanks is giving credit to God for his faithfulness, his power, his might, and his sovereignty.

In the book of Luke 17:11-17 is the story of the ten lepers that were healed by Jesus. In verse 15 and 16 one of them having seen that he was healed came back, threw himself at Jesus feet and thanked him. In verse 17 Jesus asked, were not ten healed and where are the other nine? This passage shows us the significance of thanksgiving. God is looking for our gratitude. He longs for us to go to him with thanksgiving and appreciation. Thanking him for all that he is in our lives. Look around you, there is so much to be grateful for. Do not be like the nine lepers that never came back to say thank you.

PRAYER

Heavenly Father. I come before you with a heart of thanksgiving, and I enter your courts with praise (Psalms 100:4). I am grateful for the gift of life. Almighty God, I thank you for your love, I thank you for the gift and sacrifice of your son Jesus Christ (John 3:16). I give thanks to you, and I will tell of your marvelous works (Psalms 9:1). Thank you for every day; Thank you for the food on my table, clothes on my body, and a roof over my head. I am grateful for your mercies and lovingkindness that are new every morning (Lamentations 3:22-23). Thank you for your grace and peace in my life. I thank you for provision and benefits that you provide daily (Psalms 68:19).

Thank you for the gift of life, thank you that I have seen another day. Thank you because you are Ebenezer, you have brought me this far (1 Samuel 7:12) and the work you have began in me, you are faithful to complete it (Philippians 1:6).

Blessed be your name forever and ever.

In Jesus Name, Amen.

God is looking for our gratitude.

FORGIVENESS

Isaiah 53:5 says, He was wounded for our transgression and bruised for our iniquities. The chastisement of our peace was upon him.

Forgiveness means pardon for sin. God sent his only beloved son to die on the cross for us so that we may receive the gift of forgiveness and salvation (John 3:16). The wages of sin is death but the gift of God is eternal life (Romans 6:23). It does not matter what depths of sin we find ourselves in; our loving God is ready with open arms to forgive and embrace you as a son or daughter. The bible says in Psalms 103:12 that as far as the east is from the west so far has he removed our transgressions from us. In 1 John 1:9 the Bible tells us that if we confess our sins, he is faithful and just to forgive us and purify us from all unrighteousness.

Forgiveness is a gift from God, ask of it and receive it. It is through the prayer of forgiveness that God calls you his own. It is through Salvation and forgiveness of our sins that we receive the gift of eternal life. We should also forgive others who have sinned against us according to the Lord's prayer in Luke 4:11. Jesus said in Mathew 18: 21-22 that we should also forgive others seventy times seven times in a day.

PRAYER

Heavenly Father, I cry out for your forgiveness. Thank you for the shed blood at Calvary, because through that, my sins are washed away. Forgive me of my sins and cleanse me from all unrighteousness (1 John 1:9). I ask for forgiveness for where I have stumbled, where I have failed, where I have slipped and fallen. Forgive my thoughts for moments I have doubted, forgive my actions where I have gone against your will and purposes for me. May I find mercy as I come before your throne (Hebrews 4:16)

I pray that I forgive all that have wronged me according to your word in Mark 11:25. Create in me a clean heart and renew a right spirit within me (Psalms 51:10). Despite all that I have done may I experience your mercies today (Daniel 9:9). Heavenly Father, you are forgiving and good and may I experience your abounding love (Psalms 86:5). I choose to repent, turn to you so that my sins may be wiped away and I may receive times of refreshing (Acts 3:9).

Heavenly Father, today I receive the gift of forgiveness.

In Jesus Name, Amen.

DAILY PRAYER

The Bible tells us that His loving kindness and mercies are new every morning. Great is your faithfulness (Lamentations 3:22-23) meaning with every new day, we receive fresh new mercies, with every new day we experience the faithfulness of God.

We need God each day of our very being. It is by His grace, his mercy, and his love that we are not consumed. Purpose every day ready to receive new mercies. Psalms 68:19 N.I.V versions says, "Praise be to Him who daily bears our burdens." A burden is any heavy load that weighs us down, but our loving Father is faithful to carry your burden daily. The NKJ version says who daily loads us with benefits. A benefit is a payment, profit, or an advantage. With every new day, our gracious Father has a gift for us.

God watches over us both night and day. Psalms 121 says that he does not sleep, he does not slumber because he is watching over us and because he is watching over us, the sun will not harm us by day, nor the moon at night.

PRAYER

Dear Heavenly Father. I am grateful to see another day. With this new day, may I experience your mercies and lovingkindness that are new every morning. On this day, I pray that you will load me with your benefits (Psalms 68:19). As I face this day, may you go before me, lead me, guide me, walk with me, and talk with me. I desire your presence just like Moses (Exodus 33:15) because in your presence is fullness of joy and at your right-hand treasures evermore (Psalms 16:11).

Watch over me both day and night, in my coming and in my going (Psalms 121). Keep your eyes on me as I keep my eyes fixed on you (Psalms 141:8). May this new day be full of the abundant goodness and greatness of God (Psalms 31:19)

In Jesus Name, Amen.

> *"In your presence is fullness of joy... at your right-hand treasures evermore"*
>
> *-Psalms 16:11*

<u>**PROTECTION**</u>

In the world, we are always surrounded by danger. The Bible in Psalms 91 tells that if we dwell in the secret place of the most high, we shall abide under the shadow of the Almighty; therefore, we are assured of His protection. To dwell means living a life of obedience and honor to God and living according to his word daily. When we do that the Bible assures us that

*The Lord will be your refuge and fortress.
*You will be saved from the fowlers snare and deadly pestilence.
*You are covered, and you find refuge
*You will not fear.
*No harm will overtake you.
* Angels will encamp around you.
* You will be protected.
*He will be with you when in trouble.
*You will find deliverance.
* You will have long life.

"Angels will encamp around you.

You will be protected."

-Psalms 91

PRAYER

Heavenly Father, you are my rock, my fortress, and my deliverer (Psalms 18:1-2). The righteous run to you, and they are safe (Proverbs 18:10). I pray for your hand of protection to be over me, and may your angels encamp around me (Psalms 34:7). Keep me from all harm and watch over my coming and my going (Psalms 121:7-8); therefore, I will say you are my refuge and my strength, an ever-present help in times of trouble (Psalms 46:1).

Protect my mind, body, family, property, finances. Protect me from diseases, sickness, and accidents. Keep me from all harm and watch over my life (Psalms 121:7). Hide me in the shadow of your wings (Psalms 17:8) for in the shadow of your wings I find my refuge (Psalms 57:1). Just like Job, put a hedge around me, my family and all that I have (Job 1:10). I declare and confess that you are my hiding place (Psalms 32:7)

In Jesus Name, Amen.

"The righteous run to You, and they are safe"

-Proverbs 18:10

STRENGTH

Isaiah 40: 28-31

Strength is the power, the energy, the vigor that enables us to push through life daily. We need physical, emotional, and spiritual strength to carry us through. Life has its ups and downs, and we find ourselves loosing strength, getting weak and weary. When we lose strength, we lose the zeal to carry on and pursue life and purpose. The Bible says that he gives strength to the weary and the weak. He renews strength just like the eagle so that we can walk and not faint, run and not grow weary.

In His word, God assures us that He shall give us strength. Joshua 1:9 commands us to be strong and courageous because the Lord is with us wherever we go. Isaiah 41:10 tells us that God will strengthen us, help us, and uphold us with his victorious right hand. Psalms 18:32 God arms us with strength.

We are faced with evil, temptations, negative forces but the Bible assures us that he gives strength and protection from the evil one (2nd Thessalonians 3:3). The flesh may get weak and weary but be watchful and prayerful so that you do not give in to temptation (Mathew 26:41).

PRAYER

Heavenly Father, I look unto you for strength (1 Chronicles 16:11). When I am weak and weary. I stand upon your word that you give strength to the weary, increase power to the weak and to those that wait upon you, you shall renew their strength like the eagle (Isaiah 40:29-31). Strengthen my weak hands and stable my feeble knees (Isaiah 35:3). I pray for strength in my mind and my emotions. I pray for strength as I journey on the road of life, hold my hand along every step (Psalms 73:23). When I am weak, carry me in your loving arms (Isaiah 46:4); when I cannot go on, show me the way (Psalms 143:8). May I find my strength in you (Isaiah 41:10) because your power is made perfect in weakness (2 Corinthians 2:9-11). Even when my soul is weary and in sorrow, I pray that you will strengthen me according to your word (Psalms 119:28)

Heavenly Father, my flesh and my heart may fail but you are the strength of my heart (Psalms 73:26). I stand assured that I can do all things through Christ who strengthens me (Philippians 4:13) and my days will be filled with joy because the joy of the Lord is my strength (Nehemiah 8:10).

In Jesus Name, Amen.

John 14:27

The Bible tells us that my peace I give unto you, not as the world gives. Peace is a state of tranquility, calmness, lack of conflict and freedom from disturbance. We need peace of mind, inner peace as well as peace in our environment (home, school, work, institutions, countries, government)

The storms of life come to take away our peace. Jesus in Mark 4:35-41 was on a boat with his disciples and there was a storm. A storm that threatened their safety in the water. The disciples who were in turmoil and panic cried out to Jesus who commanded the storm to be still. God's peace surpasses all understanding (Philippians 4:7). It is beyond what we can comprehend as it gives you a calm even during a storm. It gives you the assurance that it shall be well. God always reassures us peace and in every way.
(2 Thessalonians 3:16)

For us to have peace, our mind should be fixed on God (Isaiah 26:3). The Bible also tells us to cast all our cares, all our anxiety unto God (1 Peter 5:7). We should handle all anxiety in prayer making our requests known to God (Philippians 4:6)

PRAYER

Heavenly Father, in a world of uncertainty and turmoil, I pray for your peace that surpasses all understanding (Philippians 4:7). Amid trials and tribulations, I cry out for your peace (John 16:33). You give peace to those whose minds are fixed on you, so Father, I purpose to fix my mind and receive peace from above. Give me peace amidst every storm and calamity (Mark 4:39), give me the assurance that in all things, you are on the throne, and you are in control (Isaiah 26:3). I pray that your peace will be with me always and every day (2 Thessalonians 3:16)

May your peace be multiplied unto me (Jude 1:2). Heavenly Father teach me to be still knowing that you are God, and you are in control (Psalms 46:10). I stand upon your word that there shall be peace in my land (Leviticus 26:26)

In Jesus Name, Amen.

> *"PEACE, that surpasses all understanding"*
>
> *-Philippians 4:7*

<u>RESTORATION</u>

Joel 2:25-26

Restoration means restitution or to put back to original or former state. The Bible promises us that all that was lost will be returned to us. If you experience loss, there is restoration. Loss can be material things, resources, finances, opportunities and even time. Joel 2:25-26 assures us that God will restore all that the locust has eaten, the crawling locust, consuming locust, and chewing locust. The scripture goes on to say that after that you shall eat in plenty and be satisfied.

The story of Job is a perfect example of restoration. Job having lost everything even his children received restoration according to Job 42:10. He had more in his latter days than his former days.

The Shunamite woman in 2 Kings 8:1-6 had left her home due to a famine. She returned after several years only to find she had lost everything, so she went to the king to petition for her land. The king not only restored her land but all the proceeds from it (2Kings 8:6). Even our souls need restoration, and we are assured that in Psalms 23:3.

PRAYER

Heavenly Father, I pray for restoration according to your word in Joel 2:25. I pray for the restoration of years lost, time lost, opportunities lost, finances lost, resources lost, and relationships lost. Father restore my mind, my spirit, and my joy (Psalms 51:12), restore my soul (Psalms 23:3), and all that the thief has stolen may it be restored unto me seven times (Proverbs 6:31). Heavenly Father, just like the Shunamite woman in 2 Kings 8:1-6, may you restore even land and property that I have lost. May my life be a testimony like Job that even in loss, you restored back double. Restore my health and heal my wounds (Jeremiah 30:17). Restore unto me the joy of your salvation and renew a right spirit and uphold me by your generous spirit (Psalms 51:12)

I pray believing in your name that you will restore, confirm, strengthen, and establish me (1 Peter 5:10)

In Jesus Name, Amen.

> *"Father restore my mind, my spirit, and my joy."*
>
> *-Psalms 51:12*

ENCOURAGEMENT

2 Corinthians 4:16-18

Encouragement means giving support or hope, uplifting, motivation or inspirational. In life, we lose hope, we have moments where we want to give up and encouragement is nourishment to our souls enabling us to keep pressing on and not to give up.

The Bible tells us in 2 Corinthians 4:16-18; So, we do not lose heart. Though our outer self is wasting away, our inner self is being renewed day by day. For this light momentary affliction is preparing for us an eternal weight of glory beyond all comparison, as we look not to the things that are seen but to the things that are unseen. For the things that are seen are transient, but the things that are unseen are eternal.

The word of God is encouraging us that what we go through and experience in this world is light and only for a moment (2 kings 3:18). Discouragement sets in when things do not go as planned, we experience loss, or lose hope. Troubles do not last, is what this scripture is telling us that there is glory beyond what we see.

PRAYER

Heavenly Father, may I abide in hope daily (Romans 15:13) and live according to your word in Deuteronomy 31:6 which says that you will never leave me nor forsake me. I know that all things work together for good (Romans 8:28) so help me to always remember that and to live by it that no matter what comes my way, things will work out to my favor. Almighty God, turn around things for my good and when my heart is overwhelmed, lead me to the rock that is higher than I (Psalms 61:2)

Thank you for the assurance that you go with me wherever I go (Joshua 1:9). May I be encouraged today knowing that it is impossible for you to lie (Hebrews 16:8) and what you have purposed over my life will be fulfilled no matter what comes my way. May I find encouragement in the scriptures and likewise be an encouragement to many (Romans 15:4-5). In the midst of distress may I encourage myself in you just like David (1 Samuel 30:6)

In Jesus Name, Amen.

There is glory beyond what we see.

<u>GROWTH</u>

Growth is the process of increasing in size or number. Growth is development, advancement, or progress. As humans we were created to grow. We grow physically and mentally and for that to happen, we feed our bodies and our minds.

Isaiah 54:2-3 says, "Enlarge the place of your tent,
    stretch your tent curtains wide,
    do not hold back.
 lengthen your cords,
    strengthen your stakes.
  For you will spread out to the right and to the left; your descendants will dispossess nations and settle in their desolate cities.

We create and prepare room for growth and increase. To progress in life, we need to grow especially mentally and spiritually therefore we need to invest in those areas. Read more, it will expand your mind. Spend more time in prayer and in the word, it will bring you to a place of spiritual growth.

As humans we were created to grow.

PRAYER

Heavenly Father, I pray for spiritual growth. May I grow in your ways, and deeper in your word (2 Peter 3:18). I pray for growth in my salvation (1 Peter 2:1-3) and that my roots will go deeper every day. I pray that I will be stronger in my Faith (Colossians 2:7). I pray for growth in my mind that I may perceive all that you have for me, understand your word, and apply it to my life (1 Corinthians 2:16). May I experience all that you have for me without reservation.

I pray for the stability that comes with spiritual growth as I meditate on your word. May I also flourish, bear fruit, and not wither (Psalms 1:1-3). I pray that I will abide in you as you are the vine, and I am the branch. Without you I cannot bear fruit (John 14:4-5).

In Jesus Name, Amen.

May I experience ALL that you have for me without reservations.

PROVISION AND FINANCES

Provision is supplies and resources that give us the basic needs for everyday living. Provisions in terms of money, food, shelter, clothing are provided by God through various ways like employment, family, businesses, and well-wishers.

Isaiah 48:17 says I am the Lord who teaches thee to profit. God has all the wisdom and knowledge of how to profit and increase our finances. Open your heart and mind for Him to teach you how to profit, thus increasing your finances. Provisions are everywhere and it takes one to have a teachable spirit and allow God to teach you how to profit (financial gain). Sometimes provisions can be handed to us directly, sometimes they may come in an opportunity. Embrace the opportunity and allow the Lord to teach you how to profit through it.

In the book of Daniel chapter one when the King was looking for people to serve, one of the requirements was people that were quick to understand (verse 4) because they needed to be taught the language. Daniel qualified in this position and he rose in ranks. A mind that is willing to learn and expand is a mind that will achieve much.

PRAYER

Heavenly Father, I stand on your word in Isaiah 48:17 that you will teach me to profit. I pray for a teachable spirit to learn all that you have available to increase my finances and provisions. I pray for witty and creative ideas that will generate income. Give me the mind of Christ (1 Corinthians 2:16) to think beyond my thoughts and imagination. Bless the works of my hands (Deuteronomy 28:12) and establish the work of my hands (Psalms 90:12)

I pray that as I give to your house, it will come back to me, good measure, pressed down, shaken together, and running over (Luke 6:38). Father, your word says that you supply all my needs according to your riches in glory in Christ Jesus (Philippians 4:19). I pray that that is my portion, and may I never lack finances, provision, and resources. I pray that as I seek first the Kingdom of God, all shall be added unto me (Mathew 6:33). I declare and decree that I will lack no good thing (Psalms 34:10)

In Jesus Name, Amen.

"You will teach me to profit"

-Isaiah 48: 17

WISDOM

Wisdom is understanding, knowledge, and good judgement. Wisdom gives us the ability to make good choices, sound judgment and wise decisions. Wisdom give us the ability to choose right from wrong, good from bad, profitable from unprofitable.

Proverbs 3:13-18
Blessed is the one who finds wisdom and the one who gets understanding, for the gain from her is better than gain from silver and her profit better than gold. She is more precious than jewels, and nothing you desire can compare with her. Long life is In her right hand; in her left hand are riches and honor. Her ways are ways of pleasantness, and all her paths are peace.

With wisdom comes many benefits. King Solomon when asked by God what he wanted, he could have asked for riches and wealth, but he asked for wisdom (1 Kings 3:5-12) because he knew he needed it to govern the people. Wisdom set him apart as one of the greatest kings that ever lived.

Wisdom brings forth good decisions, good decisions deter you from steering in the wrong direction in life.

PRAYER

Heavenly Father, I pray that you may fill me with wisdom. Your word says in James 1:5 that anyone lacking wisdom, let him ask, and it will be given. Give me wisdom in my decision-making and everyday life: wisdom to do the right and honorable thing. I pray for wisdom just like Solomon (2 Chronicles 1:10-12) and that through wisdom, my house will be built, I receive strength, and I can wage my war (Proverbs 24:3-7). May I walk with the wise because as I walk with them, I become wise (Proverbs 13:20)

Your word says you give wisdom and understanding (Proverbs 2:6), so I ask of it, and I receive it today. Father teach me to love, seek and follow wisdom. May wisdom guide and lead me daily and may sound judgment be my portion.

In Jesus Name, Amen.

"Anyone lacking wisdom,

let him ask,

and it will be given."

-James 1:5

PLANS

Plans are intentions, schedules, or strategies. We make plans for our day, week, month, year and even for our life, family, and work. Everyday we are governed by the plans that we make. Plans give us direction; they are our compass as we navigate through life.

The Bible says in Jeremiah 29:11 that "For I know the plans I have for you declares the Lord, plans for good and not for evil, to give you a future and a hope. We make our own plans in the natural, but God has great plans for us. This gives us an assurance that even thought things may not go as planned, God has a great design for us, for our lives and for our future.

"For I know the plans

I have for you,

declares the Lord"

-Jeremiah 29:11

PRAYER

Heavenly Father teach me your ways because your ways are better than my ways, your thoughts better than mine, and are higher than mine (Isaiah 55:8-9). Give me direction and guide me along the way (Psalms 25:4-5). May my ears be sensitive to your voice, leading me to which way I should go (Isaiah 30:21). Guide me every morning (Psalms 143:8). I trust you and I do not lean on my understanding because you make my paths straight (Proverbs 3:5-6). Through your guidance, I find my strength, and I shall be like a well-watered garden (Isaiah 58:11)

I commit my works to you for you will establish my plans (Proverbs 16:3). Father I understand that many are my plans, but your purpose shall be established (Proverbs 19:21). Give me the assurance that even when things do not go as I had planned you work all things together for my good (Romans 8:28)

In Jesus Name, Amen.

> *"Give me direction and guide me along the way"*
>
> *-Psalms 25: 4-5*

FAMILY

A family is a basic unit in society which traditionally consists of parents and their children. It is a group of people who are related by birth, marriage.

The Bible says in Psalms 133 that how good and pleasant it is for brothers to dwell together in unity, for there, he commands a blessing. Unity is essential for a family because it builds a bond. When a family is in one accord, they walk together in agreement. There are blessings attached with unity that the Lord himself commands.

In the garden of Eden God saw it not right for man to be alone therefore he created woman. This was the creation of the family unity because the first man and woman had two sons. It is God's design and purpose for families to be created. We are not intended to be alone but to be with others.

The family unit is sacred because it is our roots and our core. We branch out from families; our basic learning begins there, and families are our pillars. Having a strong unified family is key. Discord in a family causes a broken family, separation, offense, and tension.

A strong family is a pillar and a support to generations to come. Futures are birthed in families; life's path is created through the family unit. Family members also depend on each other. A grounded family is the basis of a great family.

PRAYER

Heavenly Father, I pray for my family in accordance with Psalms 71:8. Even to my old age and grey hairs, you will not forsake me until I proclaim your might to another generation and your power to all those to come. I pray that I will bring up my children in the ways of the Lord (Deuteronomy 6:6-7), obedient children with long life shall (Ephesians 6:1-3).

I stand upon your word that you are faithful keeping your covenant and steadfast love to a thousand generations (Deuteronomy 7:9). May I train up my children in the way which they need to go, (Proverbs 22:6) and they are for signs and wonders (Isaiah 8:18).

In Jesus Name, Amen.

Futures are birthed in families.

www.ingramcontent.com/pod-product-compliance
Lightning Source LLC
Chambersburg PA
CBHW051939150726
47999CB00006B/2285